MARCO MEERKAT
ALPHABET PALS

Written & Illustrated by
MERCEDES, ALEXANDRIA,
SUZETTE and NOAH TALLANT

AuthorHouse™
1663 Liberty Drive
Bloomington, IN 47403
www.authorhouse.com
Phone: 1-800-839-8640

First published by AuthorHouse 4/21/2009

ISBN: 978-1-4389-3127-2 (sc)

Printed in the United States of America
Bloomington, Indiana

This book is printed on acid-free paper.

author**HOUSE**®

Aa

Andrew

Anteater

apples around

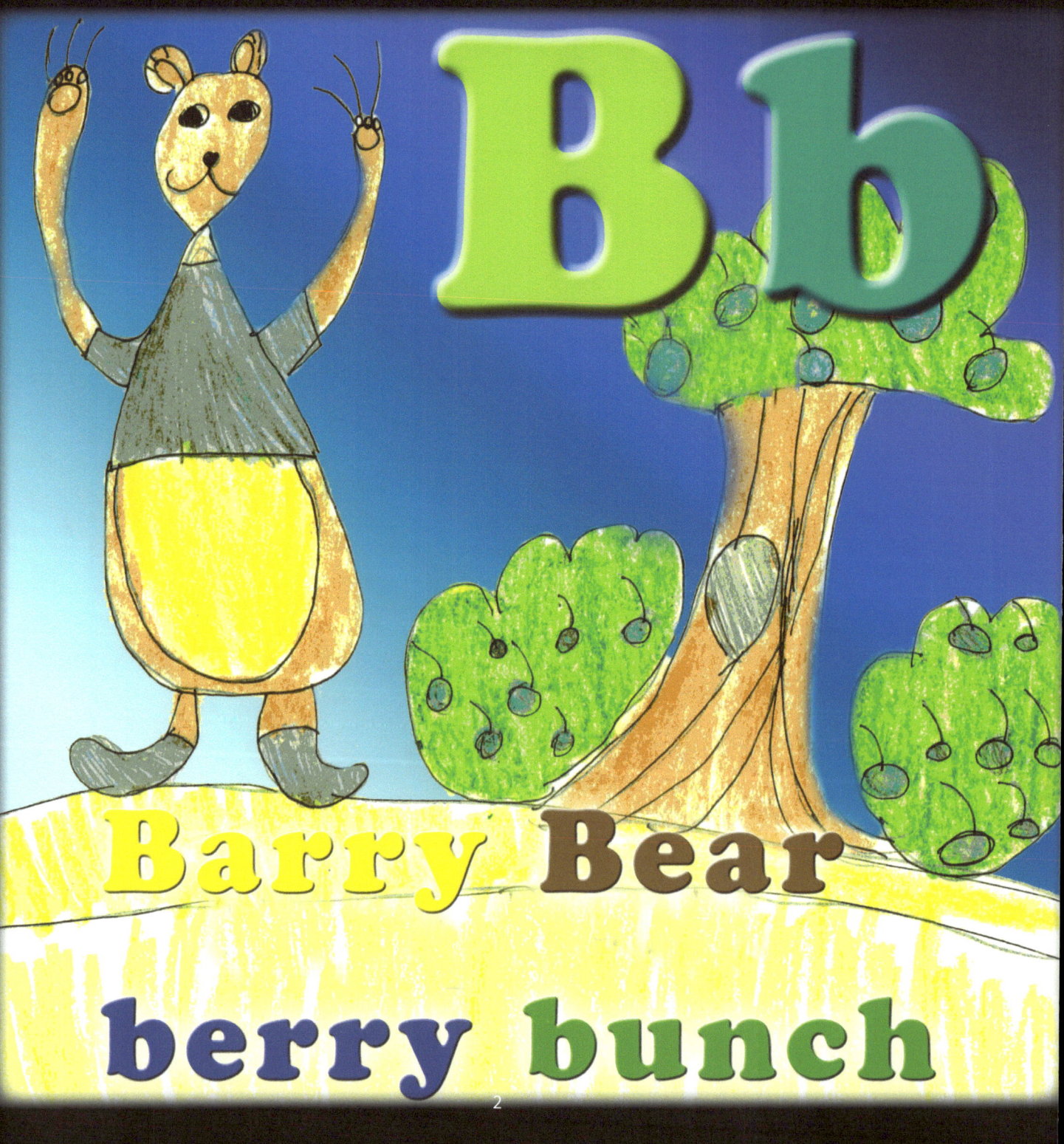

Bb

Barry Bear
berry bunch

Cc

Carrie Camel

carries cantaloupe

Dd

Daisy Dolphin

doing dives

Ee

Ernie Egret

enormous egret

Ff

Fearless
Ferret

follows

fruit

Gg

Goosey Goose

gathers grapes

Hh

Hamilton Hamster

Harry Hamster

haunted house

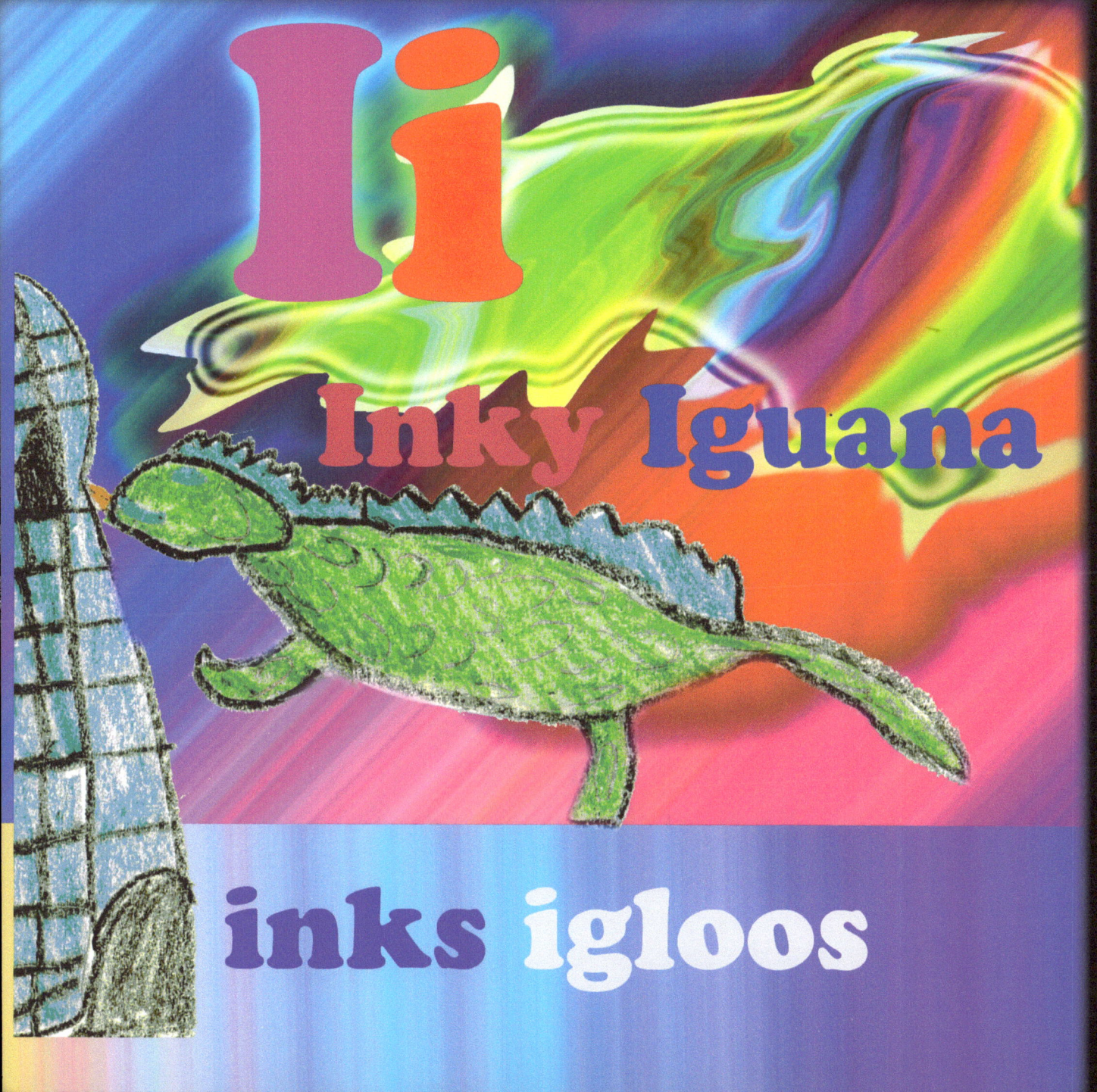

Ii

Inky Iguana

inks igloos

Jj

Jackie

Jaguar

jungle jumping

Kk

Kallie Koala

kicks kiwi

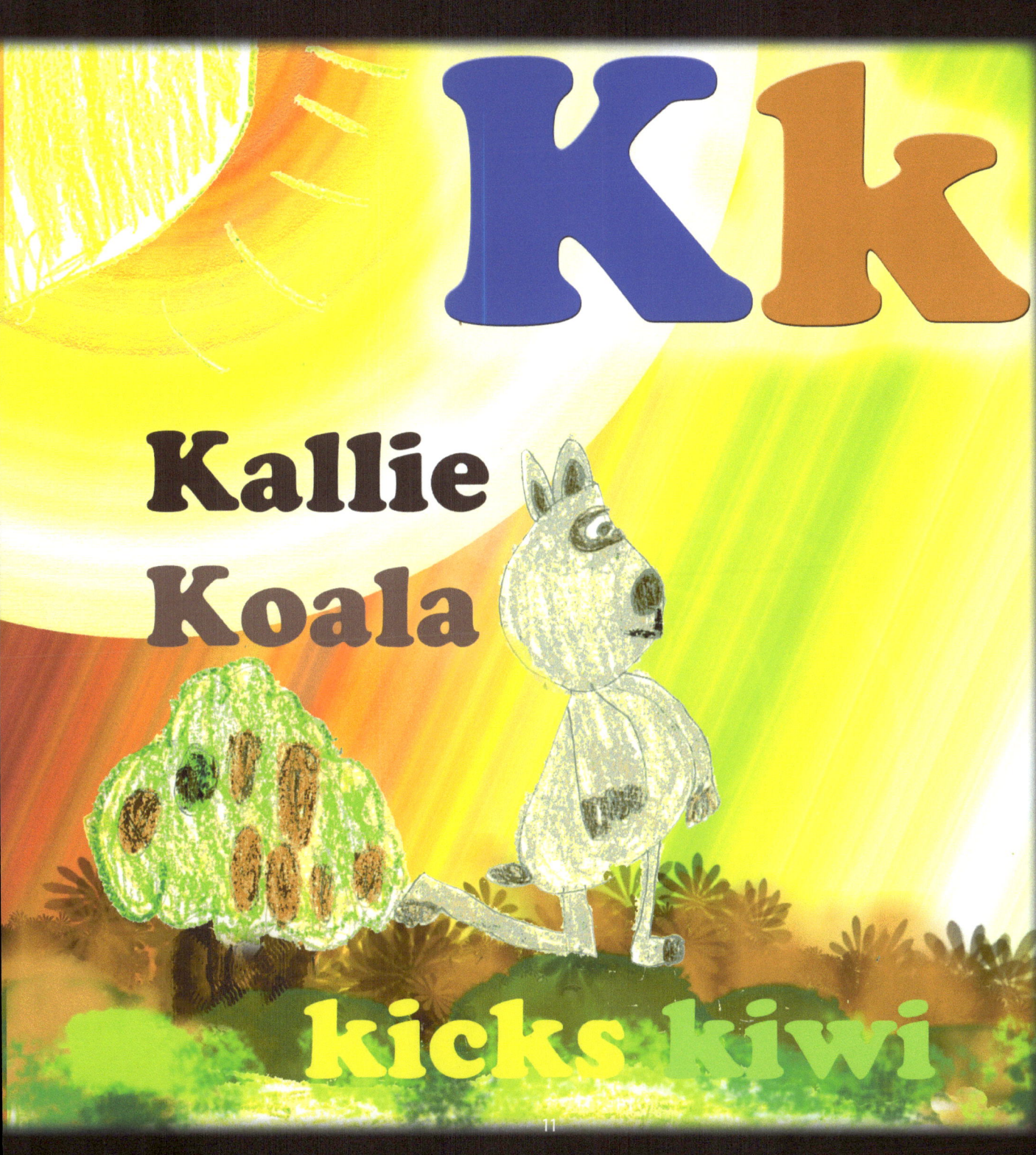

Ll

Lucy Leopard

licks lollipops

Mm

Marco

Meerkat

meets

Marvelous Man

Nn

Nanny
Nightengale

noisy neighbor

O o

Ocus Ocelot

orange ocelot

Pp

Peppy Penguin

playing pebbles

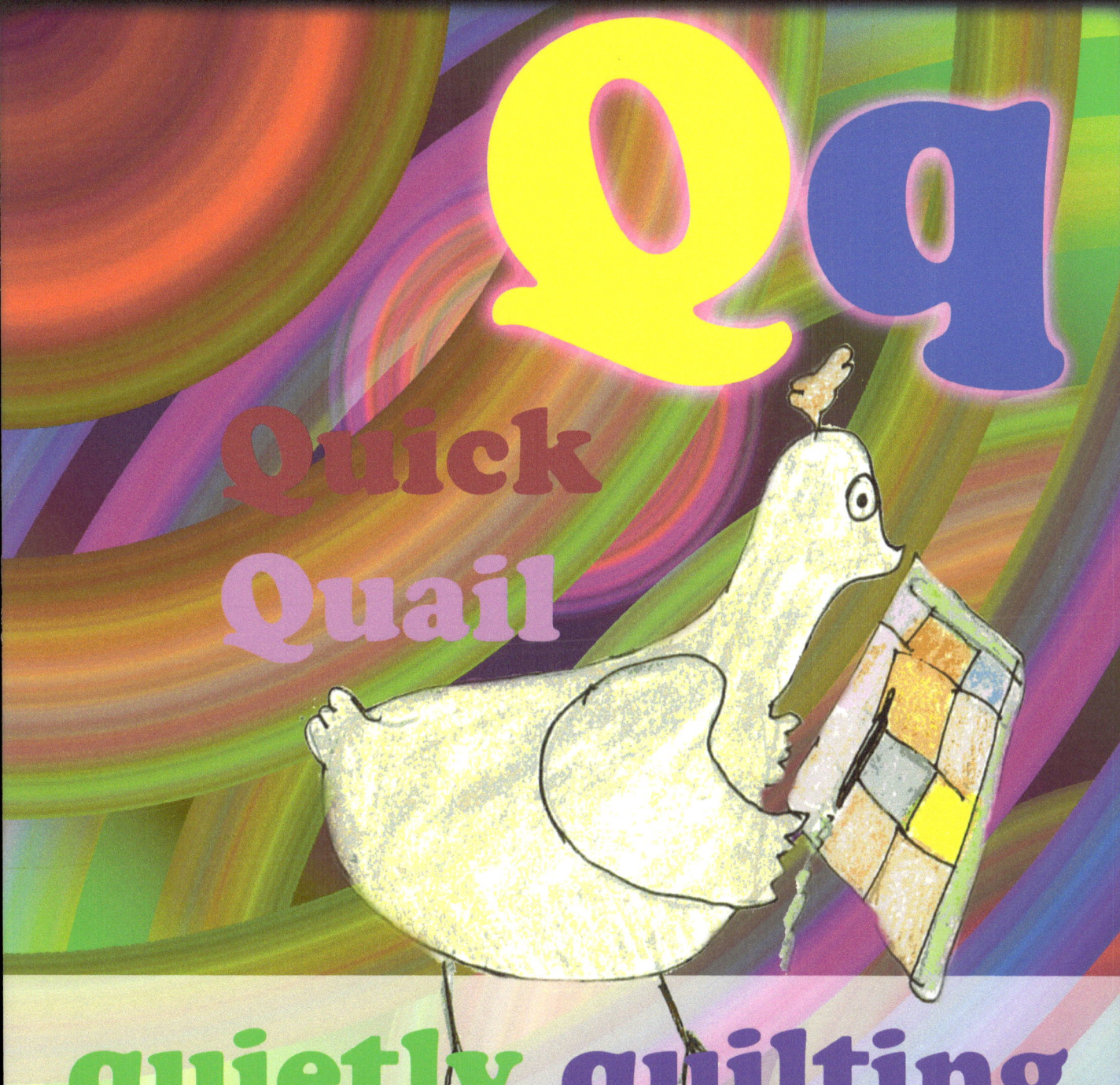

Qq

Quick
Quail

quietly quilting

Rr

Ryan
Rabbit
races
Robbie
Raccoon

Ss

Suzy
Salamander
slither slowly

Tt

Tom Tadpole

taffy tangler

Uu

Utah

Unicorn

unique

unicycler

Vv

Violet Vulture

very violet

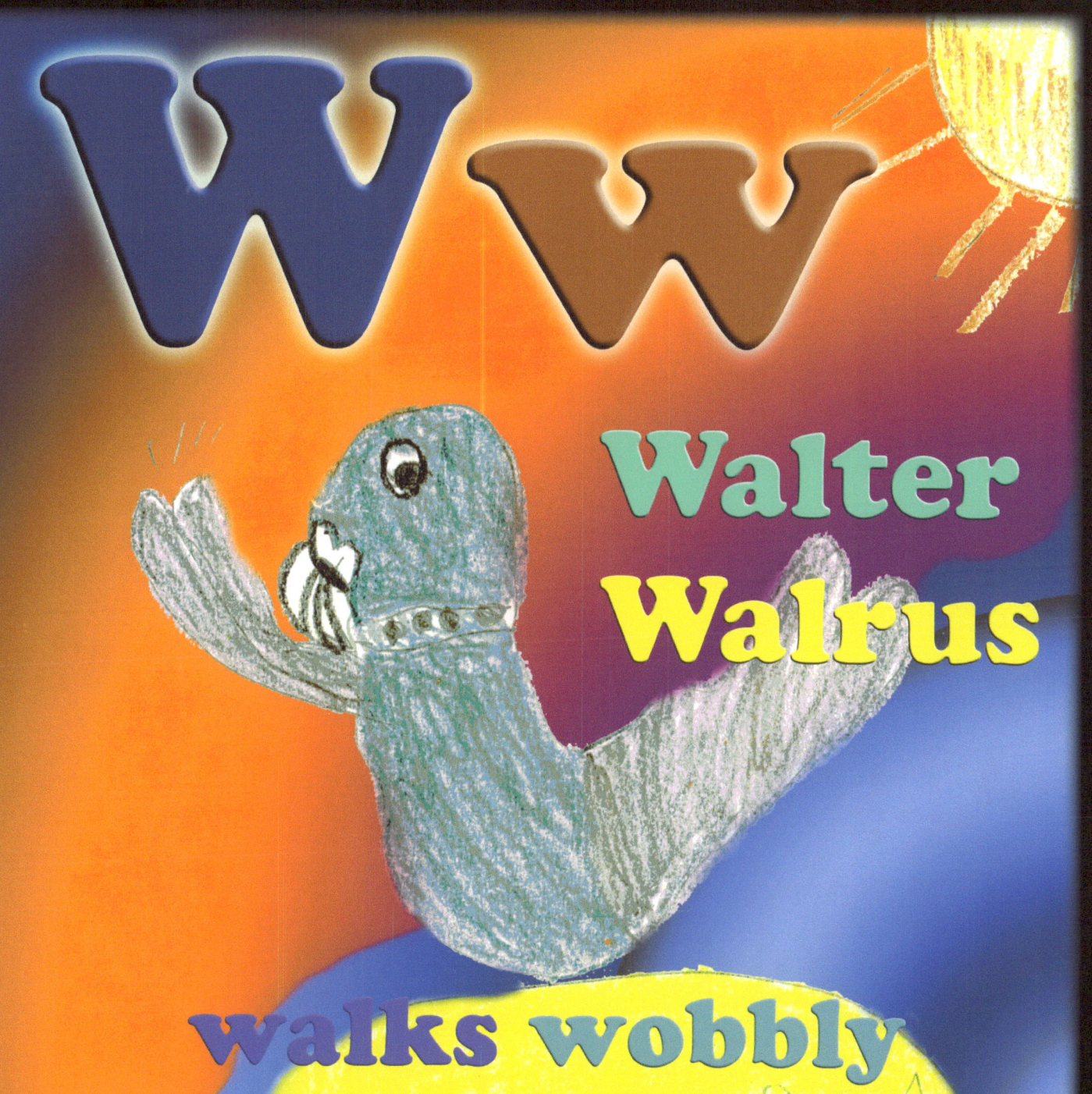

Ww

Walter
Walrus

walks wobbly

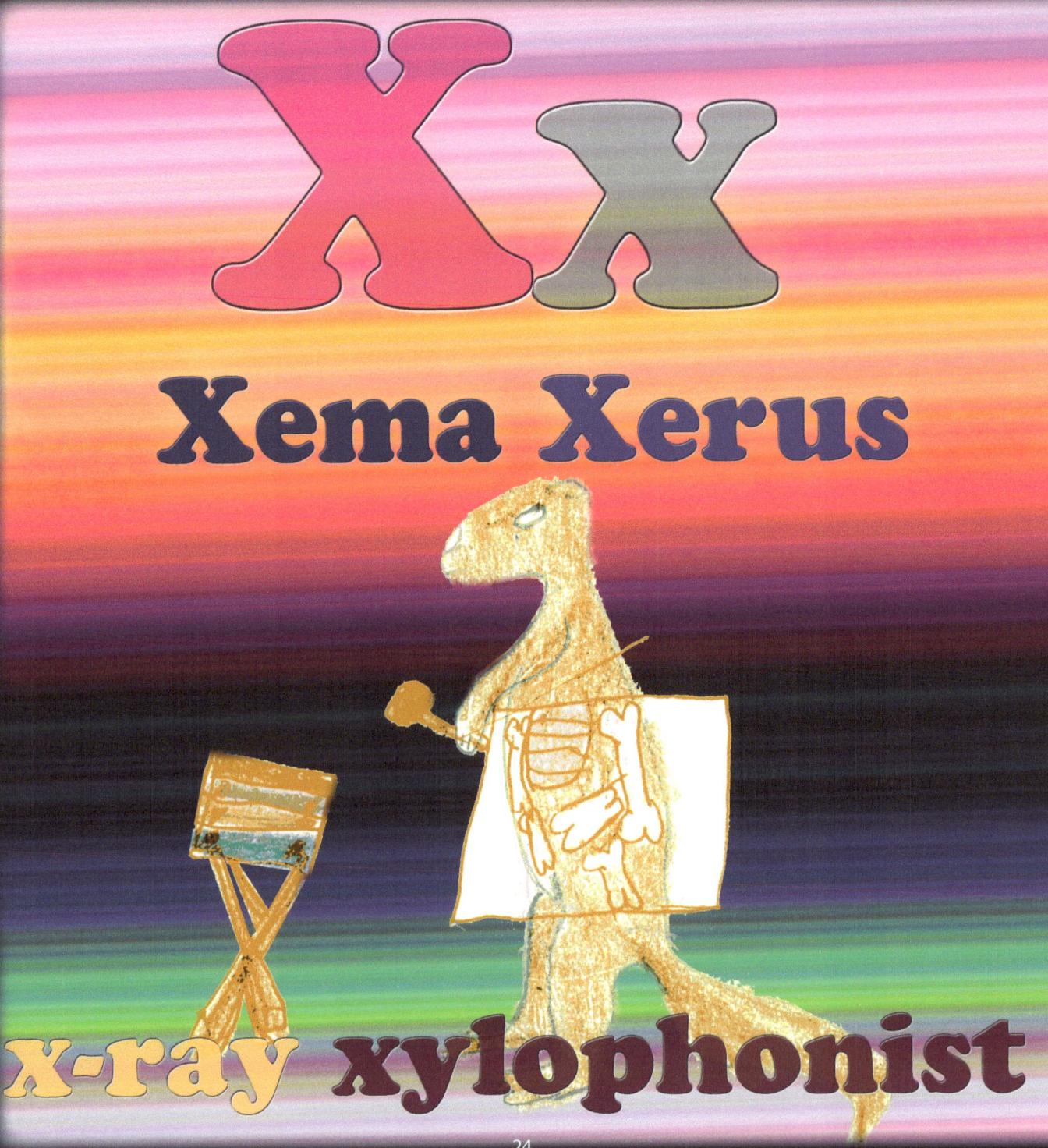

Xx

Xema Xerus

x-ray xylophonist

Yy

Yellow Yak

yawning yak

Zz

Zeta Zebra

R.i.p.

zaps zombies

Coming Soon!

Marco Meerkat

Halloweentown

Marco Meerkat

Christmas Village

The Book of Life

By Mercedes Tallant

www.ingramcontent.com/pod-product-compliance
Lightning Source LLC
Chambersburg PA
CBHW060809290526
45792CB00005BA/1583